The Secret Gardens of Cambridge

Frances Tenenbaum and Susan Twarog

The Secret Gardens of Cambridge

Copyright © 2004

by the Friends of the Cambridge Public Library
449 Broadway
Cambridge, Massachusetts 02138

Library of Congress Cataloging-in-Publication Data
Tenenbaum, Frances.
    The secret gardens of Cambridge / by Frances Tenenbaum
and Susan Twarog.
        p. cm.
    ISBN 0-9749171-0-9 (alk.paper)
    1. Gardens—Massachusetts—Cambridge. 2. Gardens—
Massachusetts—Cambridge—Pictorial works. I. Twarog, Susan Savoca. II. Title.

    SB466.M42C368 2004
    712'.6'097444—dc22

                                            2004043297

Printed in China

First printing

Book design by Jane Tenenbaum

Introduction

IN THE DEAD OF A SNOWY WINTER IN 2000 on what can only be described as an impulse, the Friends of the Cambridge Library decided to organize an open-gardens day to raise funds for the library. We gave it the literary name the Secret Gardens of Cambridge, and that first year many of the gardens were indeed "secret" to us; since they were buried under the snow, we recruited them sight unseen.

Looking back on it we can only wonder — given our carefree approach — that we didn't create a major flop. On the morning of the event, we were stunned to find a long line of ticket buyers in front of the Boudreau branch library. By the time the gardens were open, we were frantically photocopying our descriptive booklet and our tickets. Three years later, with twice as many tickets, we sold out again. The Secret Gardens of Cambridge had become an institution.

What we have learned — and continue to learn each year — is that this city contains an astonishing variety of gardens in surprising places; they reflect the diversity of the neighborhoods and the people who live here. We might expect great gardens on Brattle Street, but next to the railroad tracks? We never envisioned an elegant swimming pond and bountiful organic garden in a small backyard. And why are there so many hidden gardens on Antrim Street, in mid-Cambridge, one of the densest areas of the city? No fewer than eight Antrim Street gardens have been on our tours.

Although diversity is the hallmark of Cambridge gardens, a few similarities crop up again and again. One is the need to deal with shade, specifically shade caused by Norway maples. Another is the surprising number of gardeners whose first landscaping task was to remove the asphalt covering their yards. A third is the absence of grass, especially in the small gardens. And last is that "low maintenance" is rarely used to describe a Cambridge garden. Is it because gardening in a city is not conducive to putting in a garden and allowing it to grow without regular care? Or is it because these gardeners are such enthusiasts that what they like best about gardening is actually working at it? A few of our Secret Gardens were designed professionally, but even they are usually maintained by their owners.

This personal touch shines through so many of our gardens — it is surely why we have found such a remarkable feeling of common interests and community spirit among our gardeners. And it certainly accounts for the ever-growing number of people who visit these gardens each spring. Regrettably, not all of the gardens from our tours can be represented in this book; in many cases we were limited by the need for suitable pictures. And ultimately, of course, we were limited by space. But we are grateful to all the Secret Gardeners who have opened their gardens for the benefit of the Cambridge Public Library.

This book is dedicated to them.

Frances Tenenbaum
Susan Twarog

The Gardens

Sharon Adams

FRANCIS AVENUE

The major bones of the back garden were established in the forties. When I moved here in 1997, I had the driveway relocated to the north side of the house and replaced it with a wide border that goes from the front sidewalk to the back patio; the former carport is now a wisteria arbor. The geometry is rigid and provides a satisfying foil to the random arrangement of plants that changes almost annually. The garden reflects my interest in, or boredom with, the current trend, and it's never "done."

I enjoy searching out new colors and textures and using them in unexpected ways, often at the edge of their recommended USDA range. I especially enjoy annuals for their constant color. I do not label plants; I use them like crayons. By late summer, many of them have outgrown their space and are reaching out and grabbing passersby. It's an exuberant place.

FOUR CLOSE NEIGHBORS
ON HOLWORTHY STREET

CLOCKWISE FROM THE RIGHT

Perry and Susie Neubauer

**Christine Weisiger and
Ted Hamann**

Amy S. Bethke

Carolyn Fantasia

Simeon Bruner

BRATTLE STREET

This historic Brattle Street house was built for John Bartlett, the Harvard Square book-seller whose *Familiar Quotations* (1885) appeared in its seventeenth edition in 2002.

Under the present owner, the gardens continue to change and expand. The five major planting areas are all different — in plant material, formality, and age. The front and rear beds are more formal. Those at the street and along the front of the driveway are now over nineteen years old; the newer beds in the rear, in front of the carriage house, are in their third and sixth years. At the driveway, a line of older existing trees has been reinforced with a new hedge. A huge diversity of herbaceous material — bordering on the chaotic — is tucked everywhere. Modeled after a British garden, with a few Oriental details, the gardens have been designed and maintained by the architect-owner "with a bit of help from his friends." The garden has twice won a gold medal from the Massachusetts Horticultural Society.

Morgan and Judith Wheelock

FRESH POND PARKWAY

Just beyond the serpentine brick wall at the corner of Brattle Street is this landscape architect's garden, which appears much larger than it is. The lawn exaggerates a sense of open space, as does the sunken terrace. The layering of height in the surrounding gardens along with "borrowed landscapes" from the neighbors adds another dimension. This is a garden in the European style, reflecting the owners' love of England and France.

Karl Klaussen

Brown Street

This garden, completed in 1991, was designed by Ronald Lovinger, the head of Landscape Architecture at the University of Oregon. The entrance to the walled garden is through one of two half-moon gates. Inside, the focal point is an octagonal granite fountain surrounded by eight crabapple trees. My bedroom opens onto the garden, and the sound of falling water brings peace of mind.

Carol R. Johnson

BROWN STREET

Carol Johnson is a landscape architect who uses her garden to experiment with plants, masonry, and other details. She specializes in land form projects and in 2000 was awarded a gold medal from the Massachusetts Horticultural Society. Her garden demonstrates how to use different levels to create a variety of spaces and experiences in a small garden. The main level is raised above the street to make it feel part of the house. At the lower street level is the garage, the vegetable garden, and the outdoor dining gazebo. The top level is a deck on the roof of the garage, which provides a pleasant place to sit and look over the surroundings.

Elsa Dorfman

FRANKLIN STREET

A wisteria vine sparkling with tiny lights (and, rarely, with flowers) grows like an awning between the owner's two 1850s worker's houses. With no room for expansive landscaping, this low-maintenance city garden is quirky and informal, with something in bloom from March to November. The vine is only one of several typically entertaining garden features; most of the little plots are enhanced by the delightful sculptures of the outdoor artist John Lundstrom.

Jocelyn Giunta

LONGFELLOW ROAD

The hot, sunny area along the driveway, a perfect place for tomatoes, leads to the brick patio, where the many pots contain herbs, annuals, and some perennials. The pots are high-quality plastic made to look natural with acrylic paints and can be moved easily. Copper wire wrapped around each pot helps to ward off slugs. Two metal chairs and a small table make an excellent place to have morning coffee.

Beneath the kitchen window is a small pool made from a plastic bin and a recirculating fountain. It provides water for birds, raccoons, and possums.

A hallmark of the garden is a twenty-foot Japanese maple; other small trees include a split leaf Japanese maple near a modern sculpture and several dogwoods. The perimeter of the garden has numerous hostas and ferns, but in April it is a solid carpet of blue scilla.

Susan and Robert Filene

CHILTON STREET

Nothing visible from the front of this small house on a narrow piece of land gives any indication of the splendors to be found in the back.

"We live in Cambridge as if we were living in the country. The swimming pool was built to look like a pond, with grass and plants growing to the surrounding stones.

"We are interested in organic urban agriculture and keep experimenting to see how much food we can grow in this space. It's a challenge to cope with limited sun and many tree roots that compete for nutrients. Over the years we have discovered favorable spots for cucumbers, yellow squash, zucchini, tomatoes, pole beans, bush beans, lettuce, chard, peppers, carrots, black raspberries, and the pear trees. There isn't room to rotate crops, so we add organic soil amendments in the fall, plant winter rye, and use a large amount of compost made in six bins."

Chuck Weed and Louise Eastman Weed

AVON HILL STREET

The first time we saw what was to become our garden, there was a car stuck up to its hips in mud bordered by the concrete path that used to go to Walt's Variety, a popular neighborhood hangout in years past. We dug out the concrete and brought in a load of topsoil, which served as a mountain for our kids for a year. The garden emerged slowly, without much rhyme or reason, driven by Louise's love for plants and Chuck's for the soil.

Diane Tabor and Richard Bonarrigo

Magazine Street

The original space was a narrow, downward-sloping parking lot of parched hardpan and relentless weed growth, closely flanked by neglected buildings along each edge. First came laborious excavation, the removal and replacement of soil, and leveling and grassing over the space. The garden design evolved from the need to provide enclosure and privacy, yet openness to light, and the desire to capture a closed garden space near the house and a succession of distinct spaces midway and beyond. Most recently we added a bluestone walkway that cuts a meandering diagonal through the yard and provides two seating areas, one sunny, one shady. It terminates at a small but pleasing third garden of ornamental grasses, small specimen trees, and a combination of perennials and annuals.

Henry and Pamela Steiner

Garden Terrace

Our garden is in two parts, both tucked away and affording remarkable privacy. Its features include a high brick wall with a gate dividing the two main parts; flowering trees and shrubs; climbing roses; a small perennial bed; sculpture; and one small and one larger terraced area for summer furniture. We have worked on it for almost twenty years, building on what the previous owners began.

Mark J. Cyr
SHERMAN STREET

I grew up in this house and have been working in this soil since I was a young boy. But about 1987, after college and a tour in the Marine Corps, which included a trip to Japan, I returned to start a business building Japanese gardens. That's when I decided to add a Japanese feel to this garden without changing the original layout.

I accomplished it by adding stone formations, raked gravel areas, and other Japanese garden elements. I also took pains to start a pruning and shaping regimen on the existing trees and shrubs, not only to bring a more Japanese look to the garden, but also to practice various techniques for training these plants.

Jo and Mike Solet

BERKELEY STREET

The Tuscan elements in our garden — poppies and irises, basil, rosemary, and green peppers — are a suitable match for this 1862 Italian villa, which was built to house the Berkeley Street School for Girls. A grand American elm anchors the front garden. The mother of the king of Thailand once lived and studied at the school.

The previous gardener, Gabrielle Keyes, lived here for nearly seventy years and left us wonderful soil enriched with oyster shells gathered at her Wellfleet property. She was mad for scarlet runner beans and had riots of them climbing ladders up the sides of the house. Behind our house is a shade garden and a small fish pool with a fountain that splashes to cover city noises. The fish live in the pool all winter; a pump moves the water so it does not freeze solid.

In search of my mother's garden, I found my own.

Alice Walker

Karen Lewis

PUTNAM AVENUE

My passion for gardening is a lengthy affair and always evident wherever I've lived. Although the land around this house is quite limited, I designed new garden areas of raised planting beds to expand the garden, with the cedar pergola across the driveway to provide shade for woodland plants and vines. The orientation of the garden beds provides a great mix of sun and shade for different planting groups, with green foliage of contrasting texture and scale alongside indigenous flowering plants. Having filled the driveway with a garden, each season I enjoy the colorful changes as they unfold.

Jane Richards

ANTRIM STREET

I think of my garden as a shady oasis in the midst of an urban environment. I designed it myself (with the aid of my husband and children) to be enjoyed by both adults and children.

The garden has a variety of beds both at ground level and raised. They are on three sides of a stone dust patio, which serves as a play area for the children and a gathering place for adults and the family. No grass is tolerated; the children are encouraged to pluck each blade that may grow. On the fourth side is a raised deck with an old red brick pathway leading to the cellar and the entrance walk. A wide, gently sloping stairway connects the garden to the wooden deck.

The Lander Family

FAYERWEATHER STREET

Our house was originally the Fayerweather Street School, which moved in 1999. As we turned from renovation to creating gardens, we quite literally started with bare ground: the school had two paved driveways and parking areas with only two trees and a few bushes.

We started with three very distinct spaces. The most dramatic is the birch grove that replaced the main driveway as an entrance to the front of the house. Our birch grove is a mix of Himalaya and river birch with eastern redbuds, Japanese maples, and dogwoods as understory. We included witch hazel for sunshine in February, viburnum for the birds, and masses of daffodils and scilla to announce the spring.

The second driveway is now a garden of cherry, peach, pear, and apple trees, blueberry and raspberry bushes, and perennials. Bordered by shrubs and trees, what was once the school playground is a backyard for our three children and two dogs.

Maria Sauzier and Peter Musliner

ANTRIM STREET

First there was an orchard with a farmhouse (c. 1860). Then there was an asphalt driveway and a four-car garage (c. 1930). Now the garage is an office, and between it and the back porch is a garden that combines the elements of an English cottage garden, a lavender patch in Provence, and the fruit-bearing trees and shrubs of my childhood garden in Central Europe. Most of all, what I am looking for is a riot of color and perfume for as much of the year as possible.

Virginia and William Foote

Dana Street

We have had to work with two big challenges in the garden. Several very tall trees surround the yard, including three Norway maples, which make it difficult to grow grass and out-scale the small yards of densely populated mid-Cambridge. By planting a crabapple tree and two dogwoods, we have attempted to create a more graduated scale. The tall trees do give us quite a bit of privacy. And the sound of wind blowing through the treetops also creates a marvelous sense of peace in such an urban neighborhood.

The second challenge was to block a view straight into the parking area of a condominium behind our house. Being on the slope of a hill, the car park is elevated above our property line. We opted to install an eight-foot trellis that echoes the fences in the neighbors' bordering yards. We are training ivy, clematis, and climbing hydrangea to transform it into a wall of green with white flowering vines.

Detlev and Dorothy Vagts

FOLLEN STREET

The garden surrounds the house, and though the different areas vary in feel and scale, they all feature rock compositions set among a large variety of deciduous and mostly evergreen plants ranging from very tiny to quite large. The rear rock garden abutting the terrace contains a pool and a stream. Bloom extends from March or April to November or December. The beautiful trees in the background range from a pink dogwood on the left in the picture to the Atlas cedar on the right.

Holly Almgren and Kevin Benjamin

KINNAIRD STREET

When we moved here in 1998, the side yard was a parking lot. We removed the asphalt, trucked in organic loam, and began rototilling. It was a race against time; hundreds of pots of perennials crowded our porch, awaiting new ground. At my real estate job all day, I planted at night after our son was asleep until my husband herded me in at 1 A.M. It was like painting a giant canvas by moonlight. I did it by feel, in waves.

Half the perennials in our garden were transplanted from my garden in Redding, Connecticut, moved to our first Cambridge house in 1993, and then moved here. Certain treasures come from my mom's century-old garden in Connecticut. I grow old-fashioned favorites from childhood: bleeding hearts, foxgloves, columbine, coral bells, lilies, hellebores, ferns, phlox, poppies, peonies, and delphiniums.

Joan Krizack and André Mayer
PEMBERTON STREET

In 1998 we moved from a dense mid-Cambridge neighborhood, where we had no room to garden, to comparatively rural North Cambridge. Now, on the fraction of our tenth of an acre that is not occupied by buildings and driveway, we have several garden beds, eleven trees, and not a blade of grass.

Our main effort has been to create the garden along the back edge of the property. Neighbors warned us that nothing would grow in the area under the huge, thirsty Norway maple — the previous owner had dug a trench, lined it with plastic, and filled it with eight inches of heavy yellow pebbles — but we wanted plants. We spent the first two summers removing the pebbles and carting in soil to replace them. Our approach to selecting plants was not very methodical; some thrived while others have already been replaced.

Susan M. Carter

Francis Avenue

This house was built in a near-Federal style in 1928. The garage, shown in the photograph, looks more like a romantic carriage house, purposely designed to add a dreamy feeling to the back garden. Between the garage and the back of the house is a curved flower bed with seven varieties of pink and maroon peonies.

With pinks, purples, and whites dominating a diffusion of colors, perennials offer continuous fragrant flowering along with ease of maintenance. On the north side of the house is a small fern grove. To accentuate a colorful front entry, pink flowers accompany the climbing roses.

Deb Colburn

PEARL STREET

This quirky little garden, surrounding one of the cluster of soapworker's cottages built in 1864, is crammed with plants, chock full of vibrant color and unusual combinations. Over the years, I've changed my gardening style with the changing shade conditions. The little sticks of Bradford pear trees, planted by the city in the seventies, are now towering over the yard, and on the shadiest side I have many woodland wildflowers. The back patio is a little corner of Mexico, with bright subtropicals and lots of the folk art broken in transit to my store, Nomad.

Jay Rogers and Ted Clausen
COGSWELL AVENUE

When we bought our house on the railroad tracks in 1988, half of the backyard was paved with asphalt. To hide the train tracks, we built a covered "cloistered" walkway around two and a half sides of the property. We also found, under a mound of dirt, enough cobblestones to pave our fantasy "walkway" and edge the gardens. Today, only an occasional very loud train whistle reminds us of the tracks behind the garden.

We are not smart gardeners: we put plants too close together, can't bear to throw out extra or invasive plants, forget to fertilize and deadhead, so by the middle of the summer we despair over the jungle we've created. But at least one of us loves to weed, and the other likes to tend the lawn, so we manage to hold a slim edge over the chaos.

44

The Cambridge Zen Center Garden

AUBURN STREET

At the heart of the city block surrounded by Magazine, Auburn, and River streets, the private garden of the Cambridge Zen Center is nestled behind apartments and condominiums. The Zen Center is open to the public for meditation morning and night 365 days a year, so anyone can drop by and ask to see the garden. The residents of the Zen Center have gradually developed the garden over the years and recently installed a small pond, which is dedicated to the memory of the late Zen Master Su Bong. To the right of the koi pond is an herb garden and a vegetable patch, which supply the kitchen with tasty ingredients for fresh summer meals. On the far end is a Japanese stone garden surrounded by exotic evergreens with a hand-polished wooden bench where one can relax and listen to the fusion of rustling grasses, cars, and neighborhood basketball games.

Susan Yanow and Phillip Sego

Norfolk Street

This part of the city originally housed workers from the glass factory in East Cambridge — we've found many remnants of melted glass in our yard. The 1846 Greek Revival house was carefully placed in the northeast corner of the lot, leaving most of the garden with a southern exposure. We have tried to create an oasis in our urban garden, with color in the front to share with our neighbors and a backyard landscape that blends flowers and vegetables, bulbs and fruit trees, in an ever-changing display. The fruit trees are so prolific (123 pounds of pears in 2001) that we have listed our occupation in the city census as "farmers"!

Amy Meltzer

Antrim Street

I am an artist and love playing with color in the garden. Facing the street are sunny, colorful perennial beds, which at their peak are crowded with roses, peonies, iris, clematis, dianthus, heathers, veronicas, lavender, campanula, flax, evening primrose, and more.

A brick path leads under a rose arch to the backyard. We left the concrete slab of an old garage as a basketball court for our boys, replaced the chain-link with a wood fence, and tucked a lawn and small flower beds around our back porch. An area that is partly our backyard and partly the front of a neighbor's was designed with the cooperation of four households. It includes flowering trees, shrubs, ground covers, and hundreds of bulbs that bloom from March into June.

Meredith Leshkowich

ANTRIM STREET

This small garden becomes more secluded and tranquil each year thanks to the shade of nearby trees. Multiple tones of green accentuate the delicacy of flowering perennials and draw the eye to their individual beauty. The quiet and coolness provided on hot summer afternoons more than make up for the absence of colorful flower beds. The relative ease of upkeep for these shade-loving plants is a definite advantage. The search for plants that will thrive in this environment is an ongoing project that provides excuses for trips to the New England Wild Flower Society's Garden in the Woods and many far-flung garden centers. Every year brings a surprise to see which plants have made it through the winter and settled into their new home in Cambridge.

Maria and Michael Hanlon

BLAKESLEE STREET

Our garden consists of every inch of shady land around a two-family house bought in 1993. At the start, it had many problems: a small, sloping lot with very little privacy; heavy, clay soil; a thicket of Norway maples …

In creating our garden, I wanted a space that both my wife (who was brought up in the tropics) and I (a professional gardener) would respond to. With its large-leaved perennials, shrubs and trees, the garden feels much bigger than it actually is. Although shady, it appears lush and verdant.

Ruth Butler and Carl Kaysen
Holden Street

When we purchased our house in 1994, we were happy with the privacy made possible by a big yard, assuming we could hire someone to cut the lawn and bring in a company for annual pruning. But a big piece of earth is seductive and demanding. One of us became an amateur gardener. Every year something new goes in — a small ornamental tree like our Japanese maple, the stewartia, a crabapple, and a paper bark maple. After a visit to Kyoto, the single big tree behind the garage got axed to make way for a small Asian garden. So much shade has made rhododendrons, hollies, ferns, and hostas our best additions. But I wanted flowers; how to start? Last summer a friend helped us with a little entrance flower garden, and now we look forward to building on that.

Katharine VanBuskirk and John Scibetta
CHESTER STREET

This garden emerged as we tended the asphalt-afflicted one-third acre of urban earth around our home. In 1998, between our backyard and some huge yews in front, lay a patch of pavement that an appraiser gleefully referred to as parking for twelve. Envisioning something else, we attacked it with pickaxes, power tools, and finally a bobcat in 2001 to finish exhuming some land. We trucked in cedar from Vermont to build a tall pergola and create a formidable but see-through fence. Where there was once a small sea of asphalt, today koi and carp swim in two ponds. Nearby, on the aged rocks in our young efforts at Japanese-Zen gardening, colonies of fine mosses are growing.

Swanee Hunt and Charles Ansbacher

Brattle Street

The challenge for us in designing our garden was to make it as arresting as the house it adjoins. We wanted a garden that would provide us with food for our minds, hearts, and souls, using our sculptures to stimulate the spirit.

The provocative *Chance Meeting,* by the American George Segal, where three bronze figures meet at the intersection of two one-way "streets," is cause for much speculation by passersby. Equally thought-provoking is the Slovenian Tone Svetina's whimsical owl constructed out of shrapnel and cannonballs left in Bosnia after World War II. A second piece from the Balkans is the copper teapot-shaped ibrik with folk images hammered by a Gypsy artist in Bosnia, which we converted into a fountain.

Peaceful repose is the essence of the Coloradan Edgar Britton's *St. Francis* holding a bird; the birdbath nearby completes the sculpture. Our favorites are the bronze renderings of our three children by the "romantic naturalist" sculptor Kirsten Kokkin from Norway.

58

Elena Saporta and John Tagiuri

The townhouse garden of the landscape architect Elena Saporta and the sculptor John Tagiuri is arranged as a series of outdoor rooms. It has some of everything — sun and shade, perennial borders, fruiting trees and shrubs, peony and hydrangea hedges, a token lawn and wildflower meadow, a dining terrace, sculpture, a breakfast balcony, and a raised bed for vegetables and herbs. It is framed on all sides by climbing roses, clematis, dutchman's pipe, trumpet vine, wisteria, grape, kiwis, climbing hydrangea, and Boston and English ivies.

Jan Harvey

HASKELL STREET

We moved into our North Cambridge home in January 1991, and when spring came we found that we had inherited a backyard that contained a row of Norway maples, a scrubby spirea, and dirt. The front and side gardens had scraggly grass (mostly crab), a row of lilacs, and a rhododendron.

Our garden is mid-size for North Cambridge, triangular, with much competition from the maple trees. We removed two trees, had a brick patio built under the remaining ones, and installed a pergola, an arbor, and a tool shed. Little by little, all of the lawn has disappeared from both the front and rear gardens. The fences are largely covered with vines. I have installed paths with flagstones and thyme winding through perennial beds and arranged seating areas for rest and contemplation.

Laura van Dam

FAYERWEATHER STREET

Unlike the other houses on busy Fayerweather Street, ours is set far back, leaving a large rectangular front yard. What's more, the front of the house is quite close to the back of our neighbors' homes. The problem of how to get privacy while maintaining a connection with the neighborhood has been solved in several ways. The hedge of honeysuckle creates a backdrop for a colorful garden next to the sidewalk, where neighbors frequently stop to chat. Meanwhile, the hedge screens a lawn used for children's games and an outdoor sitting area. Tall bushes and an arbor covered with wisteria and clematis also separate the sitting area and home from the neighbors.

Kathryn Lasky Knight and Christopher Knight
Scott Street

Our garden is a deeply shaded quarter acre in the heart of Cambridge behind the Harvard Law School. We began it more than twenty years ago and it shall never be finished. It has an Asian feel to it and is most colorful in May, when thousands of tulips are in bloom. But a favorite time is in a February snowstorm, when the large boulders are swathed in mantles of snow and the witch hazel is in bloom.

Nancy and Fred Woods

HASTINGS SQUARE

One of the best things about our backyard is walking through the garden paths and gradually leaving the house, and the city, behind.

It wasn't always this way. For years our 150-foot backyard was a big, flat rectangle with a patch of lawn and monotonous raised rectangular vegetable beds. All we did there was store our canoes, pull weeds, and occasionally mow. Most of the time spent there felt like a chore. A waste of a great space.

About 1998, when we finally got energized, neighbors dubbed our project "the little dig," as we lugged hundreds of wheelbarrow loads of soil, gravel, stones, bricks, stone dust, and plants from the street to the backyard. First, we created a raised center area surrounded by a low stone wall. From either side of the yard, paths snake through the foliage and lead to a large stone patio we built at the base of a silver maple tree. Now, when we sit on the back patio looking at the moon on a summer night, the house is almost hidden.

Steve Carr and Louise Elving
Cottage Street

We have been cultivating our garden since 1982, when we bought our house. The house had been abandoned, and the yard was filled with a concrete driveway that led to an old cinderblock garage. We removed the driveway and tore down most of the garage, leaving part of its rear walls as ruin-esque architecture to frame a new patio. Over the years we have planted half a dozen specimen trees, including magnolia, weeping white pine, parrotia, stewartia, golden chain tree, and crabapple, and have enjoyed selecting plants that do well in the in-between conditions of small city yards. We've fenced the yard to create privacy for backyard activities while growing planting beds in front to share with the street.

Rick Gosselin and Robb Johnson

ALSTON STREET

When Rick Gosselin and Robb Johnson moved to their Cambridgeport home in 1992, the small backyard was pretty much a blank slate. Their solution began with a circular lawn, accessed along curving paths that created a generous space for mixed borders of perennials and shrubs. Given the shade and the roots of neighboring maples, plant materials continue to evolve in trial-and-error fashion. Along the way they tore down a conventional wood deck, replacing it with a brick and stone terrace that echoes the circular theme of the lawn. A few trees were added for privacy and multiseason interest, with a "grove" of three fast-growing Himalayan birches providing an attractive focal point.

David Waters and Don Sturdy

CONCORD AVENUE

David Waters and Don Sturdy, neighbors, have surrounded their two-family duplex with a series of colorful gardens. The front garden is filled in June with lupine, peonies, and columbine. Twenty-four rose-bushes line the path that wanders back to the private, fenced garden. A large bluestone terrace is perfect for entertaining, surrounded by raised shade gardens in whites and blues. Both men love to entertain, using the space as a large outdoor living room accessible from the house by a series of French doors. A separate outdoor dining area has a large table constructed from an eighteenth-century barn door. Tucked in various corners is a granite-curbed cutting garden, a potting area, and quiet benches for reading. A small pond fills the space with the sound of falling water.

Harry Shapiro and Pamela Winters

ORCHARD STREET

In 1993, we first walked through the front gate and down the path that led to a hidden country-style cottage under the trees — and we knew we were home. What we didn't know was how much the garden would teach us about plants, work, transformation, and appreciating the unexpected.

When we started, we had lots of big ideas about what we wanted our garden to be. We learned how to create "rooms," expanded our seating areas, and experimented with a lot of plants before finding ones that would survive in our dry, shady conditions (created in large part by an imposing cluster of Norway maples). Sometimes our ideas would work, sometimes not, and after a few years we began to suspect that the garden was paying no attention to us at all (much to the dismay of our inner control freaks).

Now, season to season, we appreciate how it changes on its own, and we watch and listen and help where we can. And so, after ten years of planning and planting, we have our sanctuary in the middle of the city. No matter how trying the day, the birds, the squirrel, and surprises from the garden are always there when we come home.

Amy Domini

DANA STREET

The house was built in 1841 and the facade is still original. The front of the house and portions of the side and back-yards have been gardens for twenty-odd years, as long as I've lived here. By 1999 my children were grown and I looked out on the grassy backyard and thought to myself that there was really no reason to have grass, and so it was laid out for gardening.

I grew up in a house carved out of a larger summer place that my grandparents owned. My grandfather loved gardening, and from an early age I was indoctrinated. My reward for helping him would be a dahlia bulb or, once, a small dogwood tree we'd found in the woods.

My new neighbors have a little girl who comes to help me in the garden. When she grows a bit older, I'll start rewarding her with dahlia bulbs.

The Hooper-Lee-Nichols House
The Cambridge Historical Society
159 BRATTLE STREET

The oldest building on Brattle Street and the second oldest house in Cambridge, the Hooper-Lee-Nichols House has a 17th-century core that was remodeled and expanded into a Georgian mansion in the 18th century. Its perennial garden of mostly old-fashioned varieties was planted and enlarged by the Cambridge Plant and Garden Club in the 1980s. Tended by volunteers, the flower beds contain a variety of bulbs, as well as such shrubs as fragrant yellow azalea and spicy viburnum and such perennials as santolina, alchemilla, peonies, amsonia, and phlox. The flower beds behind the house, which are frequently in shade, include Solomon's seal and hostas.

The Longfellow House

105 Brattle Street

Schoolchildren and scholars alike visit the Longfellow National Historic Site each year, exploring the majestic 1759 house with its wealth of original furnishings, art, books, and letters. This is where General George Washington made his headquarters in the crucial early months of the American Revolution in 1775–76 and where Henry Wadsworth Longfellow lived and wrote many of his most famous poems between 1837 and 1882.

The Longfellow House has a long and rich history, but the true significance of its gardens and grounds has been revealed only in recent years. After considerable research, the National Park Service and the Friends of the Longfellow House are beginning to recapture the profusion and diversity of the plantings and landscape features enjoyed by the Longfellow family but diminished over time. This landscape recovery focuses first on the Formal Garden, an exemplary Colonial Revival design by Martha Brookes Hutcheson and Ellen Biddle Shipman. A spectacular pergola-arbor already stands in welcome to what promises to be one of the finest and most romantic public gardens in Cambridge.

Longfellow Garden, c. 1905

The Main Library
The Cambridge Public Library
449 Broadway

The Main Library was designed by Van Brunt & Howe in the style now called Richardson Romanesque. Since its completion in 1889, the building has been expanded three times, most recently in 1967 by Shepley, Bulfinch, Richardson & Abbott. The historic exterior, of Dedham granite and Longmeadow sandstone, has elegantly carved capitals, an asymmetrically placed tower, and a welcoming entrance porch. The Main Library is on the National Register of Historic Places. It sits in a park that affords users a quiet respite from the hustle and bustle of urban life.

In 1995, this traditional Japanese lantern was presented to the citizens of Cambridge by the citizens of Tsukuba to celebrate the tenth anniversary of a fruitful sister city relationship. The lantern is on the grounds of the main library.

Photo Credits

Sharon Adams: 8, 9

Holly Almgren: 7, 38, 39

Simeon Bruner: 2–3, 12, 13

Steve Carr: 68

Deb Colburn: 42, 43

Susan Filene: 20, 21, 24, 25, 63, 70, 71

Jocelyn Giunta: 19

Michael Hanlon: 14, 52, 53

Jan Harvey: 62

Robb Johnson: 69

Karl Klaussen: 15

Christopher Knight: 64, 65

Karen Kosko: 18, 23, 26, 27, 28 (right), 29, 32, 40, 41, 44, 47, 48, 49, 54, 55, 56, 57, 72, 73, 74, 75 (bottom), 76, 77, 82

Meredith Leshkowich: 51

Karen Lewis: 10, 11, 16, 17, 30, 58, 59, 67, 75 (top)

Amy Meltzer: 50

Josh Race, Cambridge Zen Center: 46,

Jane Richards: 31

Jay Rogers: 45

Elena Saporta: 60, 61, 78, 79, back cover

Maria Sauzier: 34

Jo Solet: 1, 28 (left)

Stanley Twarog: 35, 80

Dorothy Vagts: 36, 37

Michael Van Valkenburgh: 33

Louise Weed: front cover, 22

Nancy Woods: 66

Susan Yanow: 48, 49

Index